D1447479

A BANTAM PATHFINDER EDITION

TRUE OR FALSE . . .

Indians have red skins and Japanese people have yellow skins—or do they?

Dark-skinned people are basically different from light-skinned people—or are they?

"White" skin is really "white"—or is it?

Everyone has heard these statements at one time or another. But how true are they? No subject is more clouded with misinformation and misunderstanding than the subject of color. **THE COLOR OF MAN** is a survey of the facts about color, based on research by experts in many fields: biologists, anthropologists, historians, sociologists and psychologists. At a time when informed opinion must replace prejudice and propaganda, **THE COLOR OF MAN** offers an objective view of this troubled subject.

BANTAM PATHFINDER EDITIONS

Bantam Pathfinder Editions provide the best in fiction and nonfiction in a wide variety of subject areas. They include novels by classic and contemporary writers; vivid, accurate histories and biographies; authoritative works in the sciences; collections of short stories, plays and poetry.

Bantam Pathfinder Editions are carefully selected and approved. They are durably bound, printed on specially selected high-quality paper, and presented in a new and handsome format.

THE COLOR OF MAN

by *ROBERT COHEN*
with an afterword by *DR. JUAN COMAS*
Illustrated by *KEN HEYMAN*

BANTAM PATHFINDER EDITIONS
TORONTO / NEW YORK / LONDON

Coh
c. 2

RLI:	VLM 7 (VLR 6-8)
	IL 5-up

THE COLOR OF MAN

A Bantam Book/published by arrangement with
Random House, Inc.

PRINTING HISTORY
Random House edition published 1968
Bantam edition published April 1972
3rd printing
The photographs on pages 9 and 12 are courtesy of
Clay-Adams, Inc., N.Y.C.

Published simultaneously in the United States and Canada

Bantam Books are published by Bantam Books, Inc. Its trade-
mark, consisting of the words "Bantam Books" and the por-
trayal of a bantam, is registered in the United States Patent
Office and in other countries. Marca Registrada. Bantam
Books, Inc., 666 Fifth Avenue, New York, New York 10019.

PRINTED IN THE UNITED STATES OF AMERICA

CONTENTS

Chapter **1** *What Is Color 7*

Chapter **2** *Where Does Color Come From? 25*

Chapter **3** *All Men Are Brothers 39*

Chapter **4** *Millions of Dark Skins 59*

Chapter **5** *Millions of Light Skins 67*

Chapter **6** *The World of Color 75*

Chapter **7** *The Idea of Color 97*

Afterword by Dr. Juan Comas 117

CHAPTER 1/WHAT IS COLOR

COLOR is an important part of vision. Much of what we sense comes to us through our eyes, and color helps us identify what we see. We find color in the rocks, trees, houses, animals and all the other things that make up the world we live in. No matter what language we speak or what nation we belong to, we all see the sky as blue, the earth as brown, fire as red. Color is an experience common to all mankind.

Color is used throughout the world to communicate ideas and attitudes. A red traffic light means "stop" and a green light means "go" in Paris, Philadelphia and Peking alike. But the same color can also mean different things to different people. In the Western theater the color white usually means purity or goodness, while black stands for death, sorrow or villainy. In the Eastern theater, on the other hand, an actor with a white patch in the center of his face is either a clown or a liar, and black stands for honesty and integrity.

Colors not only help us to identify characters in a play and to control traffic, but they also play an important part in determining how we think about other people. There are millions of people who are convinced that having light skin makes them better than anyone whose skin is dark. At the same time, there are millions of people who believe that men should not be judged by the color of their skins. They demand equal rights for all mankind. Before

JAPAN

trying to decide whether it is right or wrong to judge people by the color of their skins, we should know something about skin color itself. And to find the facts we have to turn to science.

From a scientific point of view, color is not a standard by which to judge people. It is simply a fact. Science is the never-ending search for facts, and to the scientist color is only one of many things to be studied and analyzed. Only by considering the most reliable evidence available can we gain an understanding of what skin color means.

THE CAUSES OF COLOR

The microscopic cells of the skin contain the basic elements of skin color. If we look at skin through a microscope, we can see that it is made up of three layers. Spread about in the middle and lower layers are tiny grains of coloring material or pigment. There are five different pigments in the skin, but the one which has the most to do with its color is a black pigment called melanin. The separate grains of melanin can only be seen through a powerful microscope. They are so small that when we look at them with the naked eye they blend together and give the skin an even-colored appearance.

Everyone's skin, whether light, medium or dark in color, contains the same black melanin. We see different skin colors because the amount of melanin in the skin varies from person to person. People with dark brown or black skins have a great many melanin particles; people with medium to light brown skins have fewer; people with very light brown to white skins have only a very few.

The melanin particles are usually spread about evenly, but irregularities in skin color are fairly common. When enough melanin particles collect in one place, dark spots appear on the skin. These spots are called freckles. Freckles can be found in people of all colors, but since they show up better against a light background, they can be seen most easily in

MELANIN GRANULES

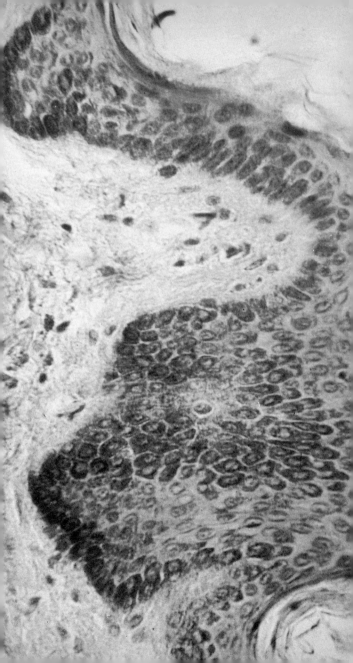

light skins.

Another pigment, yellow-orange carotene, also plays a part in skin color. The amount of carotene that a person has in his skin depends largely on what kind of food he eats. Certain foods, such as carrots, fish oils and corn, contain more carotene than others. People who eat a lot of these foods have large amounts of carotene in their skins, and their skins may have a slightly yellowish tinge; but this disappears once their diet is changed. The amount of melanin in the skin, on the other hand, usually remains the same no matter what foods are eaten. Because of this, melanin is considered a basic pigment, while carotene is not.

The skin's thickness also has an effect on its color. The top layers have no color of their own, but the thicker they are the more they lighten the colors found in the middle and lower layers. (The same thing happens with fog or mist. Fog is colorless, but it scatters and lightens the colors of things seen through it.) Since blue light is more easily scattered than red, the thicker the upper layer of skin becomes, the bluer the melanin in the lower layers appears. A man with a lot of melanin and a thick skin will be blue-black in color; another man with the same amount of melanin, but a thinner skin, will have a reddish-black color. When the skin is thin and hasn't too much melanin in it, the red of the blood underneath shows through. So people with very light skins actually appear pink in color.

Even though we use the word "white" in describing light-skinned people, from a scientific point of view no skins are really *white* in color. No matter how light a person's skin may be, compared to a piece of white paper it is not white at all. In order to have truly white skin, you would have to have no melanin and no blood. There are a few people who have no melanin in their skins, but everybody alive has blood.

People who have no melanin at all are called

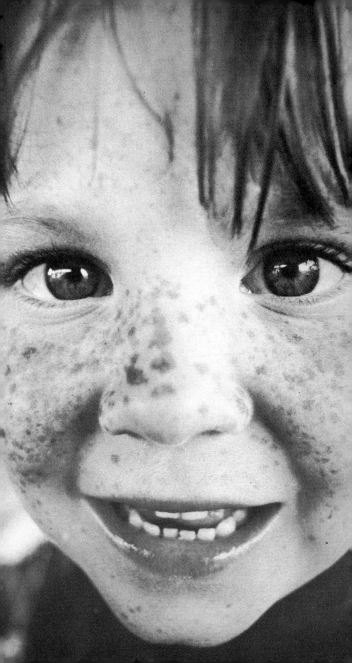

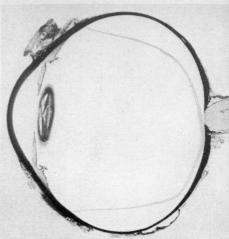

MELANIN IN THE RETINA

albinos, which means "whites." Yet even an albino's skin is light pink because the blood shows through. When we say someone is "white" we are using a figure of speech, not an accurate description.

BLACK, BROWN, YELLOW AND RED SKINS

Black and brown are truly accurate words for describing the color of many people. But "yellow" and "red" fall into the same category as "white." A person's skin is really yellow only when he has yellow jaundice or some similar disease. Many people, especially Asians, often have yellowish skins because they eat carotene-rich foods. But carotene does not give them a true yellow skin. Asians actually range all the way from light beige to dark brown, and their color depends on the same melanin as black-, brown- or "white"-skinned people's color.

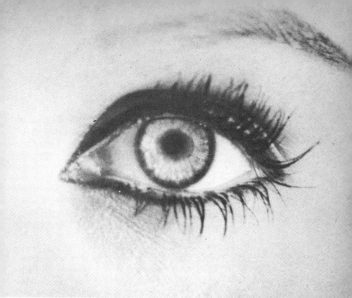

Finally, although many Northern Eurōpēans are so light that they appear pink, no one is ever really red, unless he has a very bad sunburn. The brown-skinned American Indians are often called "redskins," but that term originated because some Indian tribes used to paint themselves red for ceremonies and battles. They were no more red than the Britons who smeared themselves with blue paint many centuries ago were blue. What we see with our eyes, however, is often changed by what we are used to thinking. So we continue to talk about people being "white," "yellow" or "red." Some people think that they really see white, yellow and red skins even though they are actually seeing pinkish, beige, light brown or dark brown skins.

The color in our skin is not an accident. Like everything else in our bodies, it has its own special job to do. Scientists have discovered that melanin is very important, especially when we spend a lot of time out in the sun.

THE REASON FOR COLOR

Sunlight is made up of several parts: invisible infrared heat rays, visible light, and invisible ultraviolet rays. Most of the ultraviolet rays are stopped by the colorless upper layers of the skin. Those that get through to the lower layers of the skin could burn the sensitive sweat glands, blood vessels and nerve endings. So the skin is further protected by the grains of melanin in its middle and lower layers. The melanin absorbs the ultraviolet rays and changes them into harmless infrared heat rays.

But the melanin can stop only so much of the ultraviolet at one time. If you stay out in the sun too long, you get painfully burned. Even then, if the skin isn't burned too badly, it produces more melanin to soak up the extra ultraviolet. The extra melanin makes your skin look browner and you have a suntan.

By building up a tan through a series of short sunbaths, most light-skinned people can develop enough melanin to stay out in the sun for a long time without burning. Some people who are normally very light-skinned become quite brown after a summer out in the sun. Yet no matter how deep a tan is, it never becomes permanent. It is only a temporary protection, which fades after a few months out of the sun.

BROWN, BLUE AND PINK EYES

The skin isn't the only part of the body that differs in color from one person to the next. The eyes and hair also do. And the same elements affect their coloring.

Most of the eye is covered by what is commonly called the "white" and this covering is truly white-colored in most people. (The white sometimes looks red or bloodshot if lost sleep or some other strain has broken a few of the tiny blood vessels in it.) In the center of the white is the round iris. It can vary in color from one person to another, from a deep black to a light blue or green. In the center of the iris is the pupil. Although it looks black, the pupil really has no color. It is only the opening through which light enters the eye so that we can see.

In the eye, as in the skin, melanin is the chief coloring material. But in this case, the location of the melanin is as important as the amount. In brown and black eyes there is melanin on the inside of the white and the iris, and on the front of the iris as well. In blue eyes, the melanin is found only on the inside. While the white of the eye is opaque and lets no light pass at all, the colorless tissues of the iris do let some light through. They scatter and change the colors in much the same way as the colorless upper skin layers do. So when we look at eyes that have melanin only on the inside, the iris appears blue rather than brown or black. Similarly, the sky looks blue because the atmosphere scatters the light passing through it. If you go high enough in a rocket and get away from the earth's atmosphere, the sky is black. When the eye has melanin on the outside of the iris, as well as on the inside, we see the melanin's true black or brown color.

The melanin is usually spread evenly on the iris. When it is spread unevenly, variations in coloring occur. A close look at the eye may show darker and lighter lines of color radiating outwards from the pupil. Sometimes the melanin is evenly spread on the inside of the iris, but is unevenly spread on the outside. This produces all the various shades of blues and browns. Or there may be circles of uneven coloring. Then we get an iris with, for instance, a green inner area and a brown outer edge. Eyes are usually either blue-green (that is, with melanin only on the inside of the iris) or brown-black (with melanin on both the inside and the outside), but there is an almost infinite number of colors possible—hazels, beiges, grays, ochers, violets and various patterns of two or more colors. There are even cases where a

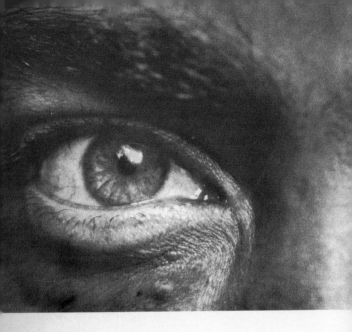

person has, say, one blue and one brown eye. Most human beings, however, have dark brown or black eyes. We will discuss the reasons for this later.

Albinos, who have no melanin, have pink eyes. As with the blood underneath their skins, the red blood inside the eyeball shows through. The colorless tissues of the iris lighten this red to pink, but it can still be seen as red through the pupil opening. So albinos have deep red pupils and pink irises.

The melanin in the eye also has an important job to do. The iris keeps the strength of the light entering the eye at the best level for good vision. It does this by narrowing the pupil opening when the light is too strong and widening it when the light is weak. But the iris is not completely light-proof itself. Light may leak through when there is not enough melanin to keep it out.

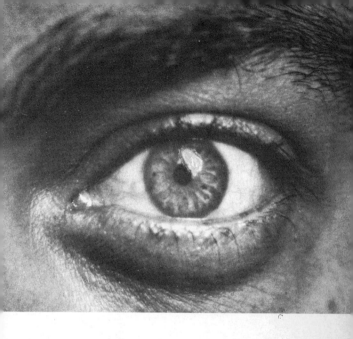

When the melanin is doing its job properly, the only way that light can come in is through the pupil opening. The melanin on the iris acts like the black coating on the iris of a camera, which keeps stray light from the film. And light leaking into the eye—except through the pupil opening—interferes with good eyesight just as light leaking into a camera spoils the film.

Since dark eyes have melanin on both the inside and the outside of the iris, they are thought to be more light-proof than light-colored eyes. Because of this, many brown- and black-eyed people seem to see a little more clearly than blue- and green-eyed people when the light is extremely strong. Away from bright sunlight the difference may not be important, but in the mountains or at the beach, people with light-colored eyes seem to be bothered more by the sun.

Besides the melanin on the iris, there is melanin behind the retina—the light-sensitive tissue at the back of the eye which changes visual images into nerve signals that go to the brain. This melanin absorbs the light rays after they have been properly focussed and changed into nerve signals. It does this before the rays can be reflected around inside the eye and make false images. People who have little pigment in their eyes suffer from weak eyesight. Light leaks through the iris and bounces off the back of the retina inside their eyes. Albinos, who have no melanin at all in their eyes, are often forced to wear special glasses in order to see even under normal lighting conditions.

BLONDS, BRUNETTES AND REDHEADS

As in the skin and eyes, melanin is also the most important coloring material in the hair. But hair sometimes has a red-gold pigment as well.

Each hair consists of a center section, a middle area and a scaly outer skin. When there are only a few melanin particles in the middle area, the colorless outer skin softens the brownish-black color of the melanin so much that the hair appears blond. When both the middle area and the center section of each hair are filled with melanin, the hair appears brown. And when the center section is packed with melanin the hair is black. Hair becomes white or gray when there isn't any melanin at all in the center or middle sections.

In all the more than three billion people in the world, there are only three basic hair colors—black-brown, where only melanin is present; red, where only the red-gold pigment is found; and a mixed type, where melanin and the red-gold pigment are found together. In the brown-black type, we find all the various shades from jet black through dark, medium and light brown to blond, depending on the

amount of melanin. The red type ranges from deep red through the medium and light reds to the palest golden-red. The mixed type goes from black, where the red-gold pigment is hidden by a large amount of melanin, through dark, medium and light red-browns to a very light reddish-beige. When peroxide, perspiration, salt water or sunlight bleaches out the melanin in the mixed type, the hair becomes both lighter and redder. The less melanin there is, the more easily the red-gold pigment is seen.

Hair can be bleached or dyed to change its color, but as with suntans, after a time the true color returns as new hair grows in.

Some permanent color changes take place naturally. Blond hair in children often darkens as they grow older. And hair of any color tends to turn gray or white in old age. Whether you are a black-headed Eskimo or a red-headed Scotsman, your hair will most likely become gray as you get older. The hairs containing melanin or red-gold pigment are replaced by unpigmented, colorless ones, which look white or gray.

While most of the people in the world have dark brown to black hair, many Northern Europeans and Scandinavians have blond or light brown hair. Red hair appears more often in Scotland than anywhere else. The largest percentage of blonds is in Sweden. Even in Africa, Asia, Polynesia and the Americas, where people almost always have dark hair, there are many exceptions. For example, when the first Europeans landed in Australia they found that many of the dark-skinned natives were blond. Some redheads have been reported among the normally black-headed tribes of Central Africa. And many Northern Europeans and Scandinavians have brown or black hair.

Dark skin and dark hair generally go together. The

NORTH AMERICA

20

same holds true for light skin and hair. But hair color seems to be only a side effect of skin color. No one has yet discovered if hair color has any particular job to do.

THE FIRST FACTS

These then are the first facts that science can tell us about human color: Color depends on the amount of melanin in the skin and eyes and hair, and dark skin and dark eyes give better protection from strong sunlight than light skin and eyes. So far, it would seem that dark coloring is better than light. But that is not the whole story. There are more facts that we have to consider.

AFRICA

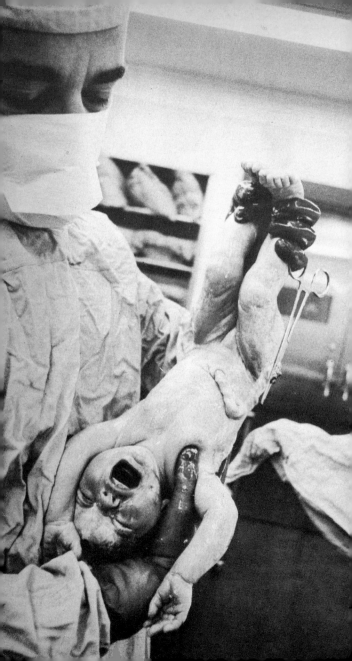

CHAPTER 2/WHERE DOES COLOR COME FROM?

WHERE does man's color come from? How is it passed on from parents to children?

For centuries, people believed that color, and everything else that we inherit from our parents, was passed on through the blood. Many people still do. You will hear them talk about a "full-blooded Negro." By this, they mean someone whose parents were both dark-skinned. In the same way, a "half-blood" has one light-skinned and one dark-skinned parent. And a "quarter-blood" has one dark-skinned and three light-skinned grandparents.

The "blood" theory seemed to make sense, but it was not based on facts. The facts became known when scientists began to study heredity, the way in which mental and physical traits are passed on from one generation to the next.

FROM PARENTS TO CHILDREN

The first thing that scientists discovered is that the blood of the parents does not mix, and cannot mix, when a child is conceived. A child is conceived when one of his father's sex cells is joined to one of his mother's sex cells. This new cell grows by dividing into millions of cells to become the baby that is born some nine months later.

Scientists also found that sex cells themselves do not contain any blood. The baby's blood is produced by his own body, inside the womb, when the neces-

25

sary blood-making cells appear. And this does not happen until some time after conception.

Although the mother carries her baby inside her body, her blood never comes into contact with the baby's. The walls of her womb will not allow blood cells to pass through. In fact, if they did, the mother's blood would injure the baby and might even kill him.

So blood has nothing to do with heredity. Once this fact was understood, the scientists began to study the sex cells. Inside the nucleus or center of each cell, they found tiny stringlike elements which they called chromosomes. (This means "things that can be stained"—referring to the fact that chromosomes have to be stained before they are visible under a microscope.)

Next they discovered that the chromosomes contain thousands of smaller particles which they called genes. The word comes from a Greek word meaning "race" or "tribe." It was well chosen, because genes carry the pattern of each new generation of human beings.

Some genes, for instance, determine the sex of the baby. Others control such things as the shape of his nose and the waviness of his hair. And some genes control the color of his skin and hair and eyes.

Genes are responsible for everything that a child inherits from his parents.

CHROMOSOMES AND GENES

Most of the cells in the human body have forty-six chromosomes, although sometimes there are more. But one kind of cell has only twenty-three—the sex cells. So when a sex cell from the father combines with a sex cell from the mother, the new cell has the forty-six chromosomes it needs.

The chromosomes are arranged in pairs. Half of each pair comes from the father, the other half from the mother. And the genes we inherit—from 40,000 to 80,000, scientists believe—are arranged in pairs in the same way. Because of this, a child cannot in-

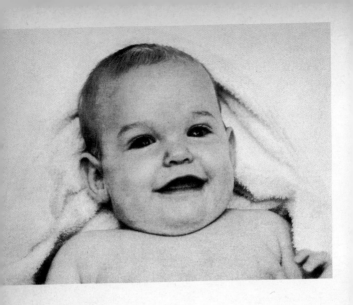

herit all of his traits from one parent, since only one half of every pair of chromosomes and genes comes from each.

Scientists think that six to eight genes are "color" genes. How do they work?

Imagine, for a moment, that there are only two types of color gene—a "dark" gene that produces dark skin and a "light" gene that produces light skin. When both parents have only light genes, they give their children pairs of light genes and the children are light-skinned. Parents with only dark genes have dark-skinned children with pairs of dark genes.

So far, this is no different from the blood theory. Two dark-skinned parents produce dark-skinned children just as two cans of black paint, mixed together, produce black paint. Two light-skinned parents produce light-skinned children just as two cans of white paint, mixed together, produce white paint.

If a light-skinned parent and a dark-skinned parent have a child, the child gets a "mixed" pair of genes and is medium-colored. The blood theory can explain this too. A can of white paint and a can of black paint, mixed together, produce gray.

But what happens if two medium-colored parents, with mixed genes, have children? According to the blood theory, they will have medium-colored children. Two cans of gray paint produce gray paint. But that is not what happens. Medium-colored parents often have children of several different colors. And only genes explain what occurs.

One child may get a light gene from each parent and be light-colored. Another may get a dark gene from each parent and be dark-colored. And a third may get a mixed pair of genes and be the same color as his parents.

Reality is much more complicated than this simple example. There are not just two kinds of color gene, but anything from six to eight. This means that a child can inherit any one of at least thirty-six mixtures of genes from his parents.

Of course, he can still get two light genes and be light-colored, or two dark genes and be dark-colored. But if the parents have mixed genes themselves, the children will probably be of many different shades of color. And since most families do have mixed genes—unless they have been cut off from the rest of mankind for generations—each child is usually a slightly different color from his brothers and sisters.

LIKE AND UNLIKE

When the parents have mixed genes, it is possible for some of their children to be darker than the darker parent and some to be lighter than the lighter parent.

In the southern United States, "white" slave-owners often had medium-colored children by their dark-skinned slaves. Sometimes the light-skinned son of the light-skinned slave-owner and his light-skinned wife had children with one of the medium-colored women. These children would never be darker than their medium-colored mother nor lighter than their

father. They could never be as dark as their dark-skinned grandmother, because only one parent had a mixed pair of genes.

People of any color can have albino children, but this has nothing to do with normal genes. Albinos occur only when the gene that controls melanin is damaged. And that is not a color gene.

This kind of change is called a mutation. It is an accident and usually serves no useful purpose. Sometimes, for instance, a child will be born with six fingers on each hand. He may pass this trait on to his children. And an albino may have albino children. But most mutations die out because they are not an improvement. They can even be harmful, as in the case of an albino. Some mutations, however, are valuable and these are the ones that remain.

NORTH AMERICA

AFRICA

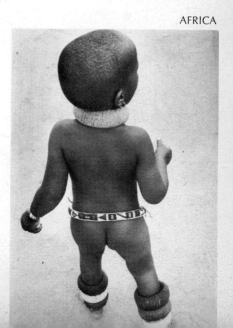

31

NORTH AMERICA

Occasionally a mutation takes place in a color gene. A child could be born with a completely different color from his parents. However, it is not likely to happen. All of the pairs of color genes would have to change at the same time for the difference to be noticeable.

Children usually inherit a mixture of their parents' traits, but they do not all inherit the same mixtures. The only people who inherit exactly the same mixture of genes are identical twins.

Ordinary twins or triplets or quadruplets are born when more than one of the mother's sex cells are fertilized at the same time. But since these children come from separate male and female cells to begin with, they are no more alike than any brothers or sisters. They are simply born at the same time.

Identical twins, on the other hand, are born from the same cell. Instead of growing in the usual way, the fertilized cell splits in two. This produces two identical fertilized cells, and each of them grows separately. Since each of the two children born from these cells gets exactly the same genes, they are the same in every way. As they grow up, differences in the lives they lead may give them different personalities, but identical twins always remain similar in their looks and coloring and other inherited traits.

The number of identical twins is extremely small—so small, in fact, that we can say that most of the three billion or so people living today have their own special combination of genes. The chances are trillions to one against two people ever being born with the same pattern. Very few people ever look exactly alike. No one—not even an identical twin—ever thinks and acts in exactly the same way as someone else. People belong to the same faiths, speak the same language, vote for the same political party; people of one nation or one part of the earth share many physical traits, such as skin color. But every human being is still original and unique.

SUN AND SHADOW

Heredity is not the only thing that influences our color. Where we live and how we live after we are born are important too. For instance, our genes influence how fat or thin we are. But our weight depends mainly on how much we eat and how much exercise we get. In the same way, our skin color depends to a large extent on how much sunshine we get.

Nearly every human being has melanin in his skin. But almost everyone can produce more melanin and tan in the sun. Some people, such as albinos, have no melanin genes, or only very few. Their skin will never become darker no matter how long they stay in the sun. But nobody can get a tan unless sunlight falls on his skin.

During the cold winter months, people keep themselves covered. A group of light-colored people will all seem to be pretty much the same color in these months. But when summer arrives and they go to the beaches, some will tan darkly, some will tan lightly and a few will not tan at all. Each one has inherited a different ability to tan, but the differences do not appear until the conditions are right. An outdoors man will soon become pale if he switches to an indoor job, while a desk clerk will take on a tan after a short vacation in the sun.

SUNTANS AND SOCIETY

Sometimes people decide that being tanned is better than being pale. Sometimes they decide the opposite.

Centuries ago, most of the people in Europe were peasants and had to work in the fields all day. Noblemen, on the other hand, did not have to work. They stayed indoors and remained pale. You could always tell a nobleman from a peasant because the peasant had a tan. As a result, noblewomen went to great lengths to keep their skin as light as possible. A skin so pale that the veins showed was thought to be a mark of great beauty.

During the Industrial Revolution things changed. Farmers left their fields and went to work in factories, mines and mills. Working for long hours in dimly-lit factories and mine shafts made their skins pale. Wealthy people, however, could afford to travel to sunny countries. They had the leisure to laze on the beaches and get a tan. Having a tan became a sign of wealth.

Pale skin is no longer desirable. Instead of bleaching themselves white with lemon juice, many women spend their time under a sunlamp. In the last few years, the desire for a quick tan has led to the invention of pills and lotions that darken the skin artificially.

This has brought about another change. These pills and lotions can be bought by anyone at any drugstore. A rich man can spend hundreds of dollars on a vacation in the sunny West Indies and get his suntan there. But his lowest-paid clerk can have the same tan out of a lotion bottle for a few cents.

The time may not be far off when anyone can change the color of his skin as easily as a woman can change the color of her hair today.

So there are three answers to the question "Where does our color come from?" It comes from the genes we inherit. It comes from the conditions in which we live. And it can come from a bottle that we buy at the drugstore on the corner.

CHAPTER 3/ALL MEN ARE BROTHERS

"ALL men are brothers." People have been saying this in one form or another for thousands of years. Even when almost nothing was known scientifically about the human body, wise men claimed that all human beings were alike no matter what their nation or language or color might be. And today, scientists have proved that the wise men were right.

We know, for instance, that different species of animals can not mate and produce children. Yet all over the world, people of every conceivable color — light-colored Europeans, medium-colored Asiatics, and dark-colored Africans — have married and raised families. And this has been happening since man first appeared. So, whatever their color, all men must belong to the same species.

Another proof of this is the fact that the cells of our bodies are alike. Doctors can transfer skin or bone or eyes from one person to another. An African pygmy can give a blood transfusion to a light-colored Englishman and vice versa, if their blood belongs to the same group. (There are several different blood groups—A, B, AB and O are the major ones—but all of these groups can be found in all people, regardless of color.)

So all mankind belongs to one species. This means, probably, that we all have a common ancestor. Far in the dim past, perhaps a million years ago or more,

U.S.A.

COSTA RICA

NIGERIA

41

a complicated series of gene changes, or mutations, in a prehuman species produced the first human being. No one knows when or where this happened or how long it took, but today the descendants of that first human have multiplied and spread out to every corner of the earth.

Yet, although we belong to the same species, we still have many differences. Some we are born with, and some we learn.

Learned differences are called "acquired traits," because we acquire, or learn, them from the society we live in as we grow up. They include such things as language and customs. Acquired traits can be changed quite quickly if we move from one society to another. When India was part of the British Empire, many Indians learned to talk and think like Englishmen. And many Englishmen, who were born and raised in India, learned the languages and customs of Indians.

"Inherited traits" — the differences we are born with — cannot be changed so easily. They include everything from our sex to the shape of our noses and the color of our skin. And of all the differences between human beings, color is the easiest to see. When we see somebody at a distance, it is almost impossible to tell what language he speaks or what his religion is. But there is no doubt about the color of his skin.

We already know how skin color is passed on from one set of parents to their children. But how did the parents get their color? How did the different groups of human beings get their color? And why does the color vary from one group to another?

GEOGRAPHY, CLIMATE AND COLOR

The sun affects all human beings in the same way. We are warmed by its heat, we see by its light, and our skins are sensitive to its ultraviolet rays.

But because of the shape of the earth and the different climates, there are great differences in the strength of sunlight in various parts of the world. The sun is strongest at the equator because its rays strike the earth more directly there. To the north and south of the equator, the earth curves away from the sun. As a result, the sun's rays strike the surface of the earth at a sharper angle, and so they are more spread out. The farther north or south we go, the less concentrated is the strength of the sun.

The curve of the earth also means that the sun's rays have to travel farther through the atmosphere to reach the surface. To reach the poles, they have to pass through almost three times as much air as they do to reach the equator. Since the air absorbs some of the rays, the sun is much weaker as we travel away from the equator.

Climate affects the amount of sunlight that reaches the earth. Places where the skies are usually cloudy get less sun than places where the weather is usually clear. The clouds cut off some of the sunlight before it strikes the earth.

Rainfall also plays its part. Tall trees with thick foliage grow in wet lands. They block the sun, too, while the small shrubs and bushes that grow on dry plains and deserts do little to shut out sunlight. Land near a seacoast is more moist and cloudy than areas farther inland. Mountains often prevent the moist air from reaching inland areas. So the centers of the continents usually have clearer skies and stronger sunlight than the coasts.

As a result, areas such as the north of Europe normally have far less sunlight in any year than, say, Africa, India or Southeast Asia. And the peoples of Northern Europe are different in color from the peoples of Africa, India and Southeast Asia.

Scientists believe that the differences in climate have, over many thousands of years, played an important part in color differences. We will see how later.

PANAMA

EL SALVADOR

U.S.A.

U.S.A.

ENGLAND

U.S.A.

THE FIRST MAN

In order to explain the differences in color between one group of humans and another, it would be valuable to know the color of the first man. But this is impossible to find out for certain. We have parts of the skeletons of some of the earliest humans, but no one can tell the color of a man's skin from looking at his bones. Even so, scientists have been able to make some worthwhile guesses by studying the facts we have.

The earliest known traces of human life have generally been found in tropical and subtropical lands. So it seems safe to say that man first appeared in a warm region. Certainly it would have been easier to survive in a warm place, because man has no thick coat of fur to protect him from the cold.

Scientists also know that the peoples who have always lived in these warm lands have medium- to dark-colored skins and eyes and hair. For that matter, most human beings are medium- to dark-colored. These facts led scientists to believe that the first men were probably dark-skinned too. They were probably not as dark as the blue-black Central Africans, but were most likely a medium or dark brown.

MIGRATION AND MUTATION

Whatever their color, the first humans had some things that no other animals had. They did not have the fangs and claws and speed of a lion, but they did have highly developed brains that helped them to catch food and defend themselves even better. They had soft, skillful hands that could sharpen sticks into spears, chip flints into knives and axes, build traps, and do many other things that no other animal could do.

Their brains also told them how to work together. Early man found that a group working together could get things done better than one man working alone. In groups, they could hunt and trap more food. And the more food they had, the more children they could raise. The more children they had, the more new hunters there would be.

So as time went by, the number of men and the number of groups increased.

As long as the descendants of the first man lived close to one another, they remained alike in color and in other inherited traits. If there was a color mutation, the new gene would spread through the group after a time. But as the number of men grew, so did the distance between groups. They spread out to look for food. Some groups migrated for long distances. It became more difficult for people from different groups to marry. Sometimes natural barriers such as mountains, rivers and deserts separated the groups. Few people were willing to cross them again just to keep in touch with their old neighbors.

In this way, many groups were cut off from each other. There were always a few hardy adventurers who made the long journeys and climbed the mountains and crossed the deserts. But as the distances increased, the chances of a new gene passing from one group to another became smaller and smaller

Imagine, for instance, that a group of dark brown hunters grew so large that it split into two. At first, the two groups lived fairly near one another. But after several generations, the first group wandered away while the second stayed in its old home. There were no more marriages between them. Then a child was born into the first group with a mutation that gave him medium-colored skin instead of dark brown skin. When the child grew up, he had a great many children of his own. After a while, a large number of the first group would have the new gene and would be medium brown. There was no mutation in the second group, so its people remained the same dark brown color as before.

In this way, migration and mutation could have led to a new color. A traveler who saw the two groups might describe the first as "light people" and

AUSTRALIA

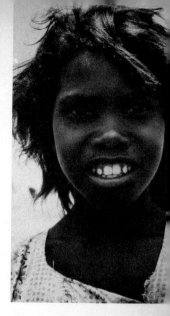
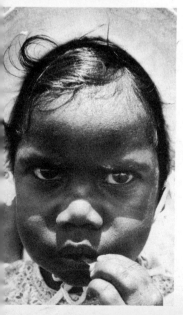

KENYA

the second as "dark people."

What actually happened was more complicated than this, but scientists believe that some of the color differences between groups of humans occurred in this way. Of course, there were many groups wandering from place to place. Sometimes they would meet other groups with new color genes. Sometimes they even wandered back to their original homes. The different genes they had developed kept mixing with other genes. As a result, the differences in color of the groups in one area were not really very great.

In any case, one child with one new gene would

not necessarily change a whole group. A change
might take place, by chance, with a few groups. But
a few such changes are not enough to explain why
the millions of people in Central Africa, for instance,
all have very dark skins, while the peoples of Northern Europe are all light-skinned.

The best explanation for what happened is called
the theory of natural selection. This theory states
that, in any area, conditions select—or favor—certain
traits over others. For instance, people who have the
right color for the area they live in have a better
chance of staying alive than people of a different
color.

NIGERIA

CHAPTER 4/MILLIONS OF DARK SKINS

LTHOUGH scientists believe that the first man developed in the tropics, they are not completely sure. Nor do they know for certain if he was dark-skinned or not. Even so, the descendants of the first man who came to live in Central Africa were very dark-skinned. They had to be in order to survive.

THE SUN AND THE HUNTER

Early man did not know how to plant crops or how to raise cattle. He found his food by hunting or by gathering wild fruit and vegetables. He spent most of his time in the open. In tropical countries, the warm sun made this possible all year round. But the sun that kept the hunter warm was also his worst enemy.

Almost any kind of clothing is uncomfortable and unnecessary in the tropics. So the early men who lived in the tropics did not cover their bodies. Year after year, the sun beat down on their naked skins as they traveled about, hunting for food. Only someone who tanned easily could avoid being burned. Even a man with a medium brown skin would be tanned almost black.

Those who could tan could stay out in the sun longer and would find it less uncomfortable. They had more time to hunt. Those who did not tan found hunting harder. And the more often they were burned, the greater their chances of getting cancer or some other skin disease.

Even newborn babies had to be able to take the strong sunlight. There were no air-conditioned maternity hospitals in those days. A mother would have her baby out in the open. The baby's skin was exposed to the sun from the instant he was born.

There was a great danger that the baby would be badly burned before he could build up a tan. But if a mutation gave a baby a darker skin, he would have a better chance to live.

We have seen that most known mutations are harmful. An albino born in a tropical climate would be at a great disadvantage. But a mutation that gave a baby darker skin would be useful. Even if he was only slightly darker than other babies, he would still have a better chance of living.

When such a baby grew up, his darker skin would give him a better chance to be a successful hunter. He would be less likely to suffer from sunburn and skin diseases.

Not only that. Being able to hunt well gave him a better opportunity to feed himself and his family. He could raise more children than a lighter-skinned hunter. And he would pass on his darker color gene to his children.

Since a dark skin is better in the tropics, the children of a dark-skinned man also had a better chance of surviving and having children. With each generation, there would be more dark-skinned people and fewer light-skinned. In time, because of natural selection, everyone in the group would come to share the new, darker color gene.

THE SUN AND THE EYE

While a man's skin needed protection from the heat of the sun, his eyes needed protection from the glare. When he aimed his spear or ax at an animal, he had to be able to see clearly to hit the target. Usually he had only one chance, and if he missed, he might have to go hungry for many days before he found another animal.

As we have seen, some scientists believe that dark eyes are better protected from strong sunlight than light eyes are. Blue eyes have no melanin on the outside of the iris, so light leaks into the eye. It seems likely, then, that a dark-eyed man would also be a better hunter in places 'where the sun was strong.

There is no way to test this idea, but most of the people in the world today have dark eyes, and it seems probable that the first men did too. Natural selection probably favored dark eyes in the tropics, just as it favored dark skins.

100,000 YEARS AT THE EQUATOR

It takes only a few days or weeks to build up a suntan. Natural selection works more slowly. It took much longer for the dark skins of people in the tropics to develop. Scientists believe it took tens of thousands of years. Sunlight did not change anyone's heredity, but it did allow the useful changes or mutations to spread.

Geneticists have worked out how long even slight changes take to affect a large number of people. Let us say that the dark skin gene we have been talking about gave a man only one extra chance in a thousand to survive. It would take 3,000 generations—about 60,000 to 70,000 years—before the one-in-a-thousand gene spread to half of the people in his group. After some 100,000 years, the light-skins would have died out and only darker-skins would be left.

Even though the lighter-skinned hunters were less successful, they would not die out quickly. The members of each group would help one another. Even the worst hunter would not starve to death because he would be given some food by the good hunters. But it was natural for the best hunters to have the most food and the largest families. Besides, the light-skinned people would also want to marry the more successful and richer dark-skinned people, and fewer lighter-skinned children would be born.

NIGERIA

But among human beings, natural selection is not the only thing that decides which traits will survive. "Social selection" is also important.

Social selection depends on the way a group of humans think and feel. It depends on the standards they set for themselves and the ideals they have. In the beginning, many of these standards and ideals are simply practical ways of surviving; but after a time, they become the means by which human beings judge each other.

We can see how this would happen with our darker-skinned hunter. At first, his darker color simply made him a better hunter. His children, too, were better hunters. Since a man's importance depended on how much food he brought in, the dark-skinned hunter would become a leader of his group. More women would want to have his children, because the offspring too would be more important in the group. So he would have his choice of wives, while lighter-skinned men would only have the second choice.

Finally, a darker skin would not merely be useful. It would also become a standard of beauty. Darker-skinned men would always find it easier to choose the wife they wanted. And they too would probably pick a dark-skinned woman because, by their standards, she was more beautiful. Gradually, because of social selection, there would be more dark-skinned children and fewer light-skinned children born.

Social selection still works today. Different countries have different standards of beauty. A man whose nose is too long or too short for his society's tastes has more difficulty in finding a wife. A woman who is too tall or too fat or too thin for her group has difficulty in finding a husband. And someone whose skin is an unpopular color may find himself shunned and despised by the society he lives in.

Unlike natural selection, social selection does not always favor the most useful traits. But fortunately, ideals and standards can be changed more easily than genes.

KENY

CHAPTER 5/MILLIONS OF LIGHT SKINS

SOME of the descendants of the first man lived in the tropics. Others migrated northward into Europe and Scandinavia, where they found that the sun was much weaker. While summer lasts the whole year round in Central Africa, in Northern Europe there are long, cold winters. For months the sun is low in the sky, and heavy clouds block the sunlight much of the time.

Anthropologists believe that, because the sunlight was weaker, the men who came to live in these northern lands gradually lost most of their genes for dark coloring. Through natural selection, the peoples of the north developed light-colored skins.

WEAK SUN AND HEAVY CLOUDS

When a band of hunters with medium brown skins migrated into the north, they found that they no longer needed protection against sunburn. In the northern lands, a light-skinned hunter could stay outside in the weak sunlight just as long as the darkest members of his group.

There was no advantage in having dark eyes either, since there was little glare. A man with light-colored eyes could aim a spear just as well as his dark-eyed neighbors.

But genes for dark skin did not simply disappear because there was less need for protection from the sun. Once again only natural selection can explain

UNITED ARAB REPUBLIC

why millions of people who live in the north have light-colored skins. Scientists believe that a light skin is better in areas where the sun is weak, just as dark skins are better in the tropics.

VITAMIN D AND COLOR

Every human being needs vitamin D to make his bones hard and strong. People who do not have enough of it suffer from a disease called rickets. Their bones become soft and weak, and their legs are twisted and bowed.

Vitamin D is made in the skin. A chemical called ergosterol, which is found in the skin, is changed into vitamin D by the ultraviolet rays of the sun.

As we have seen, melanin soaks up ultraviolet rays to stop the skin from burning. In tropical countries, enough ultraviolet rays are left to produce the vitamin D that the body needs. In northern countries, however, the sun is weaker. The skin needs all the ultraviolet rays it can get to make vitamin D. So in the north dark-colored people, with plenty of melanin, produce less vitamin D than light-skinned people.

Also, in the far north people have to cover themselves with clothes to keep out the cold. Less skin is exposed to the sun.

For these reasons, the dark-skinned hunters began to suffer from a lack of vitamin D as they moved farther north. And soft bones and twisted legs did not make good hunters. The lighter-skinned groups had a better chance of surviving. Near the equator, dark skin meant less danger of sunburn, more success in hunting and a greater chance of staying alive. In the north the opposite was the case: the lighter the skin, the more vitamin D, the stronger the bones and the greater the chance of staying alive. The different conditions in each area thus favored entirely different skin colors.

Something else also favored a light skin in the north. Women with rickets often have small pelvises. This means that the opening through which a baby

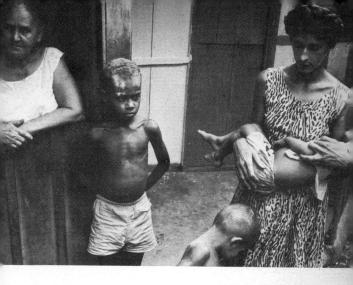

BRAZIL

is born is smaller too. Sometimes it is too small for the baby to be born normally. The mother has to have her child by Caesarean section.

Caesarean section is an operation in which a baby is delivered through an opening cut in the mother's abdomen. Nowadays, with modern hospitals and trained doctors, there is little risk. But it is doubtful that there were trained doctors thousands of years ago. There was every chance that a woman with rickets would have no children, or that she and her baby would die in childbirth.

So, as men wandered farther north into the lands of weak sunlight, they found that a light skin was better than a dark skin. Even a small amount of melanin meant less chance of surviving. Weak-boned people were not good hunters and they had fewer children. Social selection would also play its part, as it had in the warmer parts of the earth, except that in the north it favored light-colored skins. After thousands of generations, the people of cloudy

Northern Europe and Scandinavia lost most of their dark genes.

No one knows how long it took, but we do know that all the peoples who have lived in these areas for thousands of generations are very light-skinned. Scientists believe that the most probable cause was the process of natural selection.

SWEDEN

U.S.S.R.

CHAPTER 6/THE WORLD OF COLOR

THE people of the world cannot be divided simply into dark skins and light skins. Today there are almost as many shades of color as there are human beings. If all the people in the world stood in a line with the darkest at one end and the lightest at the other, it would be impossible to tell where one color group left off and the next began.

Five hundred years ago, most of the world's people lived fairly close to the places where their ancestors had lived. Color and climate were still closely connected. But since then the world has changed, and we find dark-skinned people living in lands where the sun is weak, and light-skinned people living in the tropics. And the shifting of these color groups has given modern man a new problem to face.

COLOR BEFORE COLUMBUS

During the first million years of mankind, the people of the earth wandered everywhere in search of food. For the most part, they settled wherever they found a food supply. They lost touch with everyone but their nearest neighbors. They were too busy hunting for food to think about traveling for social purposes.

Then man discovered how to grow crops and breed animals. There was a larger and more certain supply of food for everyone. And there was more time to think of other things. Villages, towns and

HOLLAND

FRANCE

MEXICO

HONG KONG

ISRAEL

cities sprang up and men moved into them from the fields. Man became civilized, and with civilization came trade. Merchants traveled from one city to another in search of business.

Between the sixth century B.C. and the eighth century A.D., the great empires appeared. The Persian, Roman, Byzantine and Arab Empires in turn spread across the Middle East, Asia, Europe and North Africa. People moved from place to place as they had never done before. Then, in the thirteenth century, the Mongols rode out from Central Asia and covered

almost half the world, from France to China. They made the distances spanned by the great empires seem almost small.

Despite all this movement, and despite trading voyages, the marching of armies and the migrations, most people still lived in or near the area in which their color group had developed. Dark-skinned Africans, medium-skinned Asians and Mongols, and light-skinned Europeans had met and mixed in the great trading centers, but the soldiers, traders and adventurers were only a handful compared with the num-

箱　　　　　　　　　　根

FRANCE

bers who stayed at home. By the time Columbus discovered America, little had changed. Climate and color were still closely connected over much of the world.

COLOR IN THE AMERICAS

America proved to be an exception. For instance, the people of Brazil were not nearly as dark as the peoples of Africa, although both regions lie across the equator. And the Indians of Canada were much darker than the English and Germans, although the sun was just as weak in Canada as it was in Northern Europe.

At first, these differences seem to cast doubt on the idea that people's color is influenced by the sun. But the explanation is simple.

Scientists believe that hardly anyone lived in America earlier than 33,000 years ago. By studying ancient campsites, arrowheads and skeletons, they have found that the ancestors of the Indians were migrating hunters who are thought to have crossed from Siberia into Alaska. From there, they moved slowly down into North, Central and South America.

These hunters probably came originally from Southern Asia. They would have had the same medium brown skins as the people who live there today. After they reached America, there was not enough time for their descendants' color to change before the Europeans came.

As we have seen, a new color gene would take about 3,000 generations to spread to half of the people in one group. But 30,000 years is only about 1,500 generations. As a result, in Columbus' day there were no great color differences between the Indians in different parts of America. Besides, many of them came long after the first migrants. The latest arrivals, the Alaskan Eskimos, have only lived in their present home for between 1,000 and 3,000 years.

So the American Indians do not disprove the theory

U.S.A.

that sun and color are connected. They are an example of how long it takes for the color of man to change.

COLONIES, SLAVERY AND MIGRATION

At the end of the fifteenth century, the nations of Europe were cut off from the Orient by the Empire of the Ottoman Turks. The Turks seized the ancient caravan routes to the East. The merchant princes of Spain and Portugal and Italy had to find new ways to bring the silks and spices of India and China.

Columbus was looking for a new route to the East when he set out across the Atlantic Ocean. He thought the islands that he discovered lay off the coast of India. It was much later that he realized he had not reached India at all, but had stumbled upon a new world.

A Portuguese navigator, Vasco da Gama, succeeded where Columbus had failed. In 1498, he sailed south around Africa to open up a new route to India. Others soon mastered the problems of ocean travel and expeditions were sent out all over the world. After hundreds of thousands of years, light-, medium- and dark-skinned men, whose ancestors had lost touch with each other, came into contact on a large scale.

During the following centuries, the great nations

U.S.A.

of Europe set up colonies all over the world. With their cannon, horses and steel weapons, Spain and Portugal conquered the Aztecs and the Incas. Their empires spread from the Americas to the Philippines. Holland took the East Indies. England fought with France over Canada and India. Wherever they conquered, the light-skinned Europeans forced the darked-skinned natives of their new empires to work as slaves on their own land.

The brown-skinned Indians of America were the first to be enslaved. But before long, light-skinned Europeans were brought over to work alongside them. Spaniards, Portuguese, Italians, Frenchmen, Scots and Englishmen were sold as slaves until a

century or two ago. The great landowners in the colonies bought prisoners from the London jails and shipped them to America. Children were kidnapped in hundreds and sold to the landlords of Massachusetts and Virginia. Many free men, faced with starvation at home, sold themselves into slavery in order to live.

SLAVERY AND CHANGE

At the beginning of the sixteenth century, the first African slaves were brought across the Atlantic to the West Indies. They were sold to plantation owners all over the Americas. Many nations joined in this profitable trade and set up slave trading posts along the West African Coast.

Between 1510 and 1860, close to 15 million Negro slaves were transported to the Americas to mix with the 6 million Europeans, both slave and free, who also lived there.

Slavery made great changes in the world of color in the 300 years after Columbus. In the New World, a whole population of color groups from different parts of the world came into being.

The eighteenth and nineteenth centuries brought more changes with the Age of the Machine. People left the land and crowded into cities to work in the factories. Populations grew. Life began to change and, with it, ideas changed. People began to question the old idea that some men were born to be rulers and some to be slaves.

So the Age of the Machine also became an age of revolution. The American and the French Revolutions were victories for freedom and equality. And all during the nineteenth century, the fight for democracy went on. In 1848 alone, there were revolutions in France, Ireland, England, Central Europe, Italy, Germany, Holland and Scandinavia.

MIGRATION AND MIXTURE

These great upheavals and the increase in population forced many people to look for new homes. They migrated everywhere in search of a better life. Between 1820 and 1935, 55 million Europeans came to America, 4 million more went to Australia, and one million to South Africa.

The Russians were also on the move. They had been spreading eastward across Siberia since the sixteenth century. After the Communist Revolution of 1917, this movement increased. Large numbers of Chinese migrated to the East Indies, to the Philippines, to Southeast Asia, to Hawaii, to the United States and to many other places. Many Hindus left India for Africa, the Fiji Islands and other places in the East. And the Japanese began to migrate in steadily growing numbers.

Tens of millions of people have migrated in the last few centuries. They have moved away from the places where their colors developed. Men and women of every color group have married and raised children, and created new shades of color that never existed before.

The greatest color mixing has taken place in the Americas. Millions of light-skinned Europeans, medium-colored Indians and dark-skinned Africans have lived closely together for the past 450 years. Scientists believe that one out of every six people living in the Americas comes from a marriage between a European and an Indian, a European and an African, or an African and an Indian. Most of the population in such countries as Mexico and Peru come from European-Indian stock. At least 80 percent of the Negroes in the United States have some European genes. And it is believed that as much as 51 percent of the descendants of the first European settlers in the United States have some Negro genes. The same kind of color mixtures have appeared in South Africa, Malaysia, Indonesia, Hawaii and India.

The change in the color patterns of the Western Hemisphere is almost completely due to the great migrations of modern times. In Europe, Africa and

U.S.A.

Asia, many people still live near the places where their color developed. But in the Americas, most people live in climates that have very little to do with the color of their skins.

History has shown that when people come together from far distant places, mankind has been better for it. New methods of growing food, new kinds of food, useful inventions and better ways of doing things have all been shared. Greece and Rome and the other ancient civilizations grew because men and ideas met there. They exchanged knowledge and information. From them came the sciences and philosophy on which our modern world is founded. This book has Roman letters and Arabic numerals

printed on paper, a Chinese invention.

Today, cities like New York, London, Paris, Berlin, Moscow, Peking, and Tokyo depend on thousands of products and ideas from every part of the world.

But although the mixing of colors of man has been a good thing in many ways, it has also created great problems. Men have begun to quarrel over color.

Many light-skinned people believe they have the right to rule the dark-skinned peoples of the earth. Millions of medium- and dark-skinned men look upon the "whites" as oppressors.

So it is not enough to know what the color of man is and how it came to be. We must also explore what the color of man means to the people of today's world.

CHAPTER 7/THE IDEA OF COLOR

I N many ways, modern science has made color unimportant. New fabrics, air conditioning and sunglasses allow light-skinned people to live fairly comfortably in the tropics. Proper diet, with enough vitamin D, allows dark-skinned people to live in good health in regions where the sun is weak. Scientific ways of producing food, building shelter and conquering disease have made natural conditions less important in man's evolution.

But color is still important in man's relations with his fellow man. Or, rather, ideas about color are important. Light-skinned and dark-skinned people all over the world are coming into conflict with each other because of these ideas.

PREJUDICE AND DISCRIMINATION

Because we inherit our genes from our parents, we tend to look like them physically. However, we do not inherit our ideas in the same way that we inherit the shape of our nose or the color of our skin. Ideas are not built into our brains at birth. They are learned as we grow up. Because we learn many of our ideas from our parents, we usually tend to think as they do. And we rarely bother to examine their ideas to see how sound and sensible they are.

For instance, if our parents teach us to dislike all those people who belong to a certain religious group or who come from a different country, we rarely try to judge the people on their merits as individuals. We learn to pre-judge them. Of course, someone can escape religious or national prejudice by changing his religion or his country, or by learning to speak without an accent. You cannot tell how anyone worships or what country he comes from by his appearance alone. But color prejudice is impossible to escape in the same way. No one can change the color of his skin.

We soon forget how, as children, we learned many of our ideas from our parents. And our parents' ideas are usually shared by the other people who surround us as we grow up—friends, neighbors, teachers and so on. So, after we grow up, we come to look upon these ideas as some sort of "common sense," not as things we have been taught. There seems to be no need to question our ideas or our prejudices, because they are so firmly planted in our minds that they seem obviously right.

THE "COMMON SENSE" OF PREJUDICE

Sometimes what we see in the world around us seems to prove that our prejudices are reasonable. For instance, those who believe that dark-skinned people are not as good as light-skinned people can point to conditions all over the earth which seem to support their belief. The light-skinned peoples of Europe and North America have more and better hospitals, schools, automobiles, bathtubs and telephones than the darker-skinned peoples of Africa, Asia and Latin America. In fact, these darker-skinned peoples not only lack modern conveniences; many of them barely have enough food to live on. If we don't take the time to find out the real reasons for these conditions, it is easy to claim that they exist because dark-skinned people are "inferior."

The real reason is that, in many parts of the world, the darker-skinned peoples have had no chance to advance to the level of the light-skinned peoples.

They have been separated because of their color and denied an equal opportunity to enjoy the freedoms of the lighter-skinned peoples. This denial is called discrimination.

In many places, color discrimination has become law. In the southern United States, for many years, dark-skinned people were prevented from attending the same schools, eating in the same restaurants or even being buried in the same cemeteries as light-skinned people. And in parts of South Africa, laws deny the dark-skinned natives the right to vote or hold political office. Other laws keep them in fenced reservations and work camps. And both dark-skinned and light-skinned people who protest against the laws are sent to jail.

Those who discriminate against the dark-skinned people claim that they are lazy, stupid, diseased or dishonest. But if darker-skinned people were naturally inferior to lighter-skinned people, then those with the lightest skins should always be the most energetic, intelligent, healthy and honest. This would mean that albinos, who have no melanin at all in their skin and are therefore the "whitest" people of all, should be better than everyone else and rule the world.

Of course, albinos do not rule the world. And the idea that we should choose our leaders only by the lightness of their skin is not very sensible. Yet prejudiced ideas about color exist in this country and all over the world. Where did they come from?

THE SOCIAL HISTORY OF COLOR PREJUDICE

Before 1650, while the United States was still an English colony, color prejudice as we know it today did not exist. Society was divided into three classes: a land-owning aristocracy at the top, a middle class of merchants and manufacturers and a lower class of peasants, servants and slaves.

The upper class of aristocrats treated the lower

NEW YORK, U.S.A.

HONG KON

LAGOS, NIGERIA

classes in the same way regardless of color. In the American colonies there were servants and slaves of all colors. Some were Europeans who had bought their passage across the Atlantic by selling themselves as slaves. Many were Africans who had been kidnapped and shipped to the colonies as slaves. The only difference between them was that the light-skinned European slaves and servants could usually earn their freedom after a number of years. The African slaves usually remained slaves all their lives and so did their children. Even so, some African slaves were freed. For instance, if the crops failed and food was scarce, they might be turned loose by their owners to look after themselves. Some of these freed slaves learned a craft or trade. In fact, a few even grew rich enough to own land and buy slaves, both light- and dark-skinned.

In the southern colonies, the warm climate was ideal for growing cotton, tobacco and other crops that needed large plantations. More and more African slaves were brought in to work in the South. By 1750, nine-tenths of the slaves in North America were in the South, and most of them were African.

By this time, the merchant middle class had grown strong enough to challenge the power of the aristocratic landowners. The middle-class philosophers declared that God had created all men equal and had given no special rights to the aristocrats. They

NEW JERSEY, U.S.A.

even questioned whether any man had the right to own another as a slave. The landowners, of course, did not want to give up either their ruling position or the slaves whose labor brought them their wealth and power. So they argued that, while all light-skinned men might be equal, people with dark skins were not really human beings. They argued that, since God had created all things, and almost all slaves were dark-skinned, God must have meant them to be that way forever.

Even though the War of Independence freed the Colonies and created the United States of America as a nation based upon liberty and justice for all, these slaves were not set free.

COTTON AND COLOR PREJUDICE

Towards the end of the eighteenth century, the price of American tobacco fell sharply. The cost of keeping slaves to tend the crop was more than the profit it brought. This was a strong economic reason for abolishing slavery. But then Eli Whitney invented the cotton gin, which cleaned cotton faster and cheaper than ever before. Powered by new steam engines, the mills in England demanded more and more cotton. So tobacco was replaced with cotton on many Southern plantations. Since cotton can best be grown by large numbers of unskilled laborers, the price of slaves shot up again. By 1830, no one in the

LOS ANGELES, U.S.A.

WASHINGTON, D.C., U.S.A.

LOS ANGELES, U.S.A.

South was talking about abolishing slavery. Cotton was king and slavery was too profitable.

Once again, color prejudice spread. But the old argument that God meant the Negroes to be slaves was no longer popular. This was the Age of the Machine and everyone was turning to the scientist, not the priest, for information. So the Southern landowners found their own scientists, who built a scientific argument in favor of color prejudice.

They said that there was not just one Human Race, but three separate races: the White, the Yellow, and the Black. The White Race was clearly superior to the others, both mentally and physically. The Black Race was the lowest, and so it was up to the White Race to take control. The best way to do this was through the system of slavery. And from 1830 to 1860, millions of words were written and thousands of speeches made to support the idea that slavery was scientifically sound.

To most people in the South, the idea seemed logical. Most of the dark-skinned people around them were ignorant, weak and unhealthy. No one listened to the scientists who pointed out that the slaves were ignorant because the landowners did not allow them to go to school, and unhealthy because they were only given sufficient food to keep them working. In the North as well, many light-skinned Americans found it easier to accept the idea than to change a very profitable system.

When Abraham Lincoln, who openly opposed slavery, was elected President in 1860, the plantation owners had to find something stronger than words. Eleven Southern states seceded from the Union rather than give up slavery. Four years later, the Civil War was over and the slave-owners had been crushed. The plantations were in ruins and the slaves had been freed.

For the first time these former slaves could vote. Many of them were elected to the legislatures of Southern states. Their children went to school and learned to read and write.

"THE WHITE MAN'S BURDEN"

Meanwhile the United States had become a world power. The factories and railroads that had won the Civil War for the North were now attracting large amounts of investment money from Europe. At the same time, a wave of settlers was spreading westward across the country. By the mid-1870's, it had reached California. The country's leaders were looking even farther. They hoped to spread America's influence into new areas—Asia, Africa and Latin America.

The ordinary American simply wanted to settle quietly on his own patch of land, but the businessmen and military leaders needed his support for their plans abroad. They began to spread the idea that it was their duty to carry a better way of life to the peoples of Asia and Africa and Latin America. It was the "white man's burden" to lead the darker-skinned peoples of the earth. Although for different reasons, the Northern leaders began to preach the superiority of the White Race in much the same way as the Southern plantation owners had done. Once they started doing this, of course, they could not attack the Southerners for doing it as well.

This gave the light-skinned Southerners the chance to take away the newly won rights of the former slaves. Gradually, the Negroes were forced back to their old position. They became poorly paid farm workers, hardly better than slaves. Those who tried to run their own farms or businesses, or who tried to vote or run for office, were threatened or murdered by secret organizations, such as the Ku Klux Klan. In the Southern legislatures, laws were passed discriminating against anyone who had a Negro ancestor—even if it was only one of his sixty-four great-great-great-great-grandparents. The old theories in favor of slavery were brought back to life and could be found in books all over the United States as the nineteenth century ended. Color prejudice became widespread again.

Only during the First World War were Negroes

finally able to start moving away from the South. In the Northern and Western states, where prejudice was not so strong, they were able to educate themselves and raise their standard of living. They began to vote and to organize themselves in growing numbers.

During the Second World War, many found work in the factories of the North and West. By the 1950's, almost half of the Negroes in the United States lived outside the South. And Americans had become disgusted with the idea of racial superiority. They had seen the Nazis use it as an excuse for murdering millions of human beings who, the Nazis claimed, were inferior.

Since then, discrimination has been wiped out in many areas by law. But laws cannot bring an end to prejudice. Only understanding can do that.

COLOR FICTION, SCIENTIFIC FACT

Through science, we have come to understand how the color of man came into being and how it spread throughout the world. Science has also shown us how our ideas are formed. And it can show us how some of those ideas, especially ideas about color, are not based on facts.

Let us look at some of the more common prejudices about color and see what science can tell us about them.

Those who believe in the superiority of light-skinned people say that dark-skinned people are not as advanced and so must not be as intelligent as light-skinned Europeans and North Americans. They say that dark-skinned people are physically weaker and naturally less healthy, and that they have more criminals among them than lighter-skinned people. On the surface, all of these things might seem to be true. But we must find out if they are true because of color or because of some other reason.

Let us take intelligence first. Psychologists, who study the human mind, have found ways to measure intelligence. Millions of people have taken intelli-

gence tests, and scientists have studied the results to find out if there is any connection between intelligence and other characteristics.

The results show that generally dark-skinned people do not score as high as light-skinned people. But they also show that better-educated people of all colors generally score higher than those who are less well-educated. And, what is most important, when light- and dark-skinned people of similar education take the intelligence tests, there is no meaningful difference between their scores.

On the whole, in schools attended by dark-skinned children, teachers are not as highly trained, classrooms are smaller and classes larger, textbooks are fewer and less money is spent for each student. No difference has ever been discovered in the brain cells of dark-skinned people that would affect their thinking. The dark-skinned students simply do not receive as good an education as the light-skinned.

In the Northern states, Negro schools are generally better than those in the South. As a result, Negro students in the North generally make higher scores on intelligence tests than do dark-skinned students in the South. In fact, since schools are generally better in the North, there are many instances of well-educated Negro students in the North scoring higher than poorly-educated white children in the South.

The highest form of intelligence, genius, can be found in people of all colors. One of the highest scores ever recorded on intelligence tests was made by a young Negro girl.

COLOR AND HEALTH

We have seen the old argument for slavery based on the idea that Negroes were physically inferior. And we have seen how false that argument was. The slave was given only enough food to keep him alive and at work, and no more. Good health and proper diet are directly connected.

This is as true today as it was in the nineteenth

LAGOS, NIGERIA

century. Medical studies show that, apart from the amount of melanin in the skin, hair and eyes, there is no known difference between the body cells of light-skinned people and those of dark-skinned people that would affect their health or strength.

It is true that all over the earth light-skinned people are generally healthier than dark-skinned people. But it is also true that all over the world, wealthy people are generally healthier than poor people. And dark-skinned people are usually poorer than light-skinned people. Because of discrimination or lack of education, they cannot find higher-paying jobs. This

111

NEW YORK, U.S.A.

means that they do not have enough money to pay for better food, housing, clothes and medical attention. Where there is ignorance and poverty, disease can almost always be found too.

Despite this, world records in nearly every sport are held by dark-skinned athletes. In boxing, said to be the world's toughest sport, seven of the last nine heavyweight world champions have been Negroes.

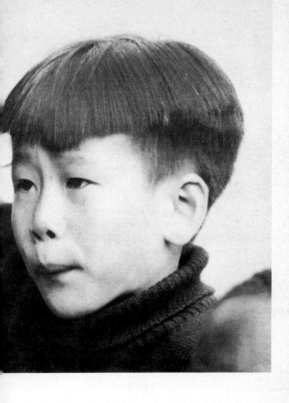

COLOR AND CRIME

It is often pointed out that crime rates are higher among dark-skinned people. Police records show that this is often the case. But the figures also show that more crimes are committed by poor people, no matter what their color is. The crime rate is also high in poverty-stricken areas where there are no dark-skinned inhabitants at all.

A poor man, no matter what his color, is far more likely to steal money, food and clothing than a wealthier man who can buy what his family needs. And the figures show clearly that the darker a man's skin, the less money he earns. This is true both in the United States and abroad. People of darker-skinned nations earn less, man for man, than people of light-skinned nations.

THE COLOR CONFLICT

It seems, then, that low scores on intelligence tests, bad health and high crime rates are connected with poverty, not with color. Scientists have not been able to discover any inborn physical or psychological reasons why a dark-skinned person cannot be as intelligent, healthy and law-abiding as anyone else —if he is given the opportunity.

It is the historian, rather than the scientist, who can show us why the lighter-skinned nations are more wealthy and powerful at the moment. It is nothing but coincidence, a matter of the history of the past few centuries. The best proof that there is no connection between a person's skin color and his mental or physical ability is that the situation is changing rapidly.

All over the world, increasing numbers of dark-skinned people are beginning to organize their own political groups and nations. They are learning the techniques and skills that once belonged only to their lighter-skinned neighbors. And, naturally enough, they are prepared to challenge those who try to hold them back. If this contest is not to end in disaster for all mankind, we must all learn to understand both the importance—and the unimportance—of the color of man.

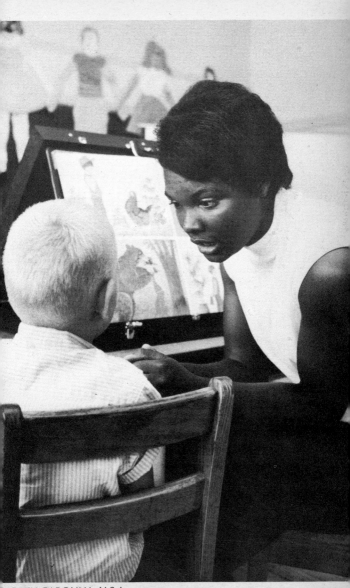

AFTERWORD
by Dr. Juan Comas
Research Professor of Anthropology,
National Autonomous University of Mexico

Throughout history, each race or ethnic group has tried to keep its sense of identity and self-importance by downgrading other groups and giving them, at best, a second place. This is particularly true when different races are distinguished by color.

The belief that there are such things as races, each one with its own unique quality, is an old one. Today, we are no longer sure that these divisions exist; at least, we do not have a definition of race that is acceptable to everyone.

Until the 18th century, people generally discussed race without feelings of prejudice. Racism began in the 19th century, possibly because of the slave trade and those who supported it. Differences of race, and especially of color, were then used—as they are still used—as an excuse for enslaving non-white peoples. This difference, which is called the color line, became the basis of the whole colonial system. Hidden behind the other motives that governed the "white" race's treatment of "colored" peoples lay, in many cases, racial prejudice.

Human beings frequently base their behavior on prejudice. We prejudge many things. But racial prejudice is the most dangerous of all, because peace between communities and nations can only be achieved through a real understanding of each other. Unfortunately, our ideas about other groups of human beings who are physically different from us are all too often based on prejudice. And ideas based on

CONEY ISLAND, NEW YORK, U.S.A.

prejudice are rarely right.

The most obvious form of racial prejudice is prejudice about color—the color of skin, of hair, of eyes. Because of it, we tend to believe that one group of human beings of a certain color has certain other qualities, although there is no logical or scientific reason for that belief. It is based on lack of knowledge, or on myths and superstition, which are fruits of ignorance.

Color prejudice makes it easier to single out, or segregate, one group in society. This can be most clearly seen in societies where a privileged "white" section of the population feels that its position is threatened. Then, the enmity between the different color groups becomes most intense.

When the "white" Europeans began to found their empires, they used color prejudice to justify their actions. "White" men were superior (in their own eyes) to "yellow," "black," and "brown" peoples. So the "yellow," "black," and "brown" peoples could be denied equality and deprived of the same political, social and economic opportunities enjoyed by those with "white" skins.

The Declaration of Independence proclaimed equal rights for all men. The Fifteenth Amendment states that "the rights of citizens of the United States shall not be denied or abridged by the United States or by any state on account of race, color or previous condition of servitude." The constitutions of most countries contain similar provisions. They can be found also in Article 2 of the Universal Declaration of Human Rights signed by the United Nations on December 10, 1948. Even so, racist doctrines continue to be one of the diseases that plague mankind. Color prejudice still plays an important role in human relations. It is still a pretext for segregating and ignoring groups of people, and unjustly depriving them of the basic human rights.

One of the strangest absurdities of color prejudice can be seen in the United States. In many places, anyone who admits to having an African ancestor, regardless of his physical appearance, is classed as a Negro. The word "Negro" in this case is not a scientific term, but a prejudiced description. Some "Negroes," in this sense, are indistinguishable from "white" men and pass themselves off as whites to escape anti-Negro discrimination. And yet anyone with the slightest amount of "Negro blood" is called a Negro.

It would be equally true, then, to say that anyone with the slightest amount of "white blood" is a white. And this would apply to almost every Negro in the United States. But because of color prejudice, federal laws on civil rights have been blocked by local laws in many states which continue to discriminate between "whites" and "Negroes."

This state of affairs is not confined to the United States by any means. The entire world suffers from the result of discrimination based on color. In South

Africa color prejudice has become the policy of the government. Apartheid, or official segregation, became law with the Colour Act of 1926 and the amendments that followed it.

In Rhodesia an equally dangerous situation exists. For many years a small "white" minority has denied a large colored majority its basic democratic rights. Rhodesia has become another focus for the threat of violence. But the same sickness is to be seen to some degree in many other countries.

In Latin America, although the color line separating Negroes, Mulattoes (half-breeds) and Indians from the "white" population is less obvious, it has been the basis for social and economic segregation.

Color prejudice also works in reverse. Many non-European peoples have shaken off their European rulers and have won their independence. At the same time, they have developed a color prejudice against the white world. In Africa, for instance, even Christianity has been split by a color line. The African Negro has set up his own black churches. The Bantu have taken down statues of the "pallid white Christ" from their churches and replaced them with black sculptures.

While we live in a world, and at a time, in which the color of human skin has become a serious threat to peace, many countries are striving to solve the

problem, to check prejudice and discrimination against groups of people because of their color. Perhaps the most important move has been made internationally by UNESCO (the United Nations Educational, Scientific and Cultural Organization). In 1950, the United Nations Economic and Social Council passed a resolution "to study and collect scientific materials concerning questions of race; to give wide diffusion to the scientific information collected; to prepare an educational campaign based on this information."

Pamphlets in many languages, lectures, press campaigns, and conferences were the results of the resolution. They were proof of the world-wide consciousness of the danger color prejudice represents, and of the urgent need for a solution. Despite these efforts, however, the fight against racism has not been successful. If anything, the problem has become worse. This has been clearly recognized by the General Assembly of the United Nations. On November 20, 1963, it approved unanimously a Declaration against all forms of racial discrimination, reaffirming the principles of its Constitution and of the Universal Declaration of Human Rights. The important paragraphs of the Declaration read:

"*Considering that the Universal Declaration of Hu-* 121

man rights proclaims that all human beings are born free and equal in dignity and rights and that everyone is entitled to all those rights and freedoms, without distinction of any kind, in particular of race, color or national origin. . . .

Considering that . . . (although international action and efforts made in a number of countries have made it possible to achieve progress in that field), discrimination based on race, color or ethnic origin in certain areas of the world none the less continues to give cause for serious concern. . . .

Disturbed by the manifestation of racial discrimination still in evidence in some areas of the world. . . .

[The Assembly] solemnly affirms the necessity of the speedy elimination of racial discrimination in all its forms and manifestations and proclaims this Declaration in order to secure by national and international measures and by teaching and education observance of the principles therein set forth."

In the eleven articles of the Declaration, discrimination against people of another color is mentioned nine times. Article 5 refers "especially to the apartheid policy," which is nothing but a legal form of racial segregation by color.

What can we do to resolve this dangerous situation?

Psychologists have shown that prejudice of any kind — including color prejudice — is not innate, not hereditary; it is learned. Children do not share the prejudices of their parents to begin with. They learn prejudice by imitation of those around them; their parents, their friends, in school, and from books, magazines, and movies.

It is almost impossible to change these attitudes in adults. Their prejudices are already formed.

We must trust to the new generations who are now growing up to solve the problem. To them passes the responsibility for the future of mankind, for the harmony between, and mutual respect for, the rights of individuals, whatever their color, through understanding.

THE ILLUSTRATIONS

pages 2-3
(left to right)
Timmy Heyman, New York; Negro girl, Harlem, New York; Japanese boy, Izu Peninsula, 100 miles south of Tokyo; Hindi girl, Benares, India

pages 4-5
(left to right)
Hausa chief, Nigeria; old woman, Brazil; photographer Edward Steichen, New York City; Italian grocer, New York City

page 6
Japanese actress in white makeup, waiting for ceremonial procession; Kyoto, Japan

page 9
Cross section of human skin, showing melanin granules

page 11
Freckle-faced girl; Fire Island, New York

page 12 left
Cross section of retina of human eye, showing melanin granules

right
Cross section of human eye

page 13
Eye of a New York fashion model

pages 16-17
Light-blue-eyed Negro (Ken Heyman's laboratory technician)

page 19
Grandmother; Switzerland

page 20 left
Hippie; New York

pages 20-21 right
Masai men; Kenya

pages 22-23 bottom
Balinese girls; Indonesia

page 23 top
Chippewa Indian; Lac Court Oreilles Reservation, Wisconsin

page 24
Newborn baby, one minute old; University Hospital, New York

page 27
Grandmother, mother, and children; Yugoslavia

page 28
Baby girl, three months old; New York City

page 30
Little girl running in Central Park; New York

page 31
Zulu child; South Africa

page 32
Girl and doll; New Jersey

page 33
Girl and doll; Switzerland

page 35
Refugee Yemenite boy and girl; Israel

page 36
Sunbathers; Fire Island, New York

page 38
Boys in front of their *favilla;* near Rio de Janeiro, Brazil

page 40 top
Three girls; Provincetown, Massachusetts

pages 40-41 bottom
Primary school children; Costa Rica

page 41 top
Boys playing in a river; Enugu, Nigeria

page 44 top
One-room schoolhouse; Pig Island, Panama

bottom	Grade school; near San Salvador, El Salvador
page 45	School children; Jerusalem, Israel
page 46 top	School children; Bronx Park, New York City
bottom	Children on schoolhouse roof; New York City
page 47	Hippies in Hyde Park; London, England
pages 48-49	Strip-farming of wheat; Montana
pages 52-53	Aborigines; North Central Australia
pages 54-55	Masai warriors; Kenya
pages 56-57	Hausa man; Jos, Nigeria
page 58	Mother and child; Ghana
pages 62-63	Hausa men with donkey caravan; near Kano, Nigeria
page 65	Seven-foot-tall Masai warrior and his wife; Kenya
page 66	Fishermen at dawn; Izu Peninsula, Japan
pages 68-69	Village street scene; near Cairo, United Arab Republic
page 71	Village women and children; Brazil
pages 72-73 bottom	Soviet gymnasts; Georgia, U.S.S.R.
page 73 top	Nursery school teacher and child; Sweden
page 74	Elderly farmer in front of a temple; Tokyo, Japan
pages 76-77	Street scene; Amsterdam, Holland
page 78	Village band; Chicumcuac, Mexico
page 79 top	Family at the beach; Cherbourg, France
bottom	Chinese family eating dinner; Hong Kong
pages 80-81	Orthodox Jews dancing; Jerusalem, Israel
page 82	Bus stop; Kyoto, Japan
page 83	Girls in Sunday clothes; Harlem, New York
page 84	French family in a park; Paris, France
page 85	Chippewa Indians; Lac Court Oreilles Reservation, Wisconsin
page 87	Indian chief at powwow; Lac Court Oreilles Reservation, Wisconsin
pages 88-89	Indian Powwow; Lac Court Oreilles Reservation, Wisconsin
pages 92-93	Sunday night traffic; Long Island, New York
pages 94-95	Helicopter view of midtown; Manhattan, New York
page 96	Street crowd; Athens, Greece

page 100	top	Park Avenue in the snow; New York Ci
	bottom	Street scene; Lagos, Nigeria
page 101		Apartment house; Hong Kong
pages 102-103		Job Corps students; New Jersey
page 104		U.C.L.A. students at a lecture; Los Angel
page 105	top	Crowd welcoming astronaut; Washingto D.C.
	bottom	Spectators at U.C.L.A.-U.S.C. football gam Los Angeles
page 109		Track meet at Madison Square Garden; Ne York City
page 111		Man chipping bark from a log; Lagos, N geria
pages 112-113		Summer camper and counselor; upsta New York
page 115		Nursery school teacher and child; Nor Carolina
page 116		Testing spacesuit to be worn by astronau on the moon; Texas
page 118		Gang fight; Coney Island, New York
page 120- 121		Children running to school; New York Ci

INDEX

Page numbers in italics refer to photographs

Abolition of slavery, 103, 106, 107
Aborigines, *52–53*
Africa, *21*, 31, 39, 41, 43, 50, *54–55*, 55, *56–57*, 58, 59, *62–63*, 65, 67, 80, 81, 86, *88–93*, 98, 99, *100*, 102, 107, 119, 120; and origin of man, 50, 59
Albinos, 12, 16, 18, 31, 36, 60, 99
   definition of, 12
   eyes of, 16, 18
   heredity of, 31
America. *See* Latin America, North America
American Revolution, 90, 103
Apartheid, 99, 120, 122
   See also: Discrimination, Segregation
Asia, 20, 39, 43, *74*, 79, 80, 81, *82*, 86, *91–93*, 98, 107

Atmosphere. *See* Climate and col
Australia, 20, *52–53*, 91
Aztec Indians, 89

Bantu tribe, 120
Black Christ, 120
Blood groups, 39
"Blood theory" of skin color, 25
   26, 28, 29, 107–108, 119–120
Bone diseases. *See* Rickets
Brazil, *38*, *71*, 86

Caesarean section, 71
Canada, 86, 89
Carotene, 10, 12
Cells, 8, 25, 26, 34, 39
China, 81, 87, 91, 93
Chromosomes, 26, 28
   number of, 26
   See also: Genes, Heredity
Civil War, 106, 107
Civilization, development of, 37
   75, 80, 81, 87–91, 92, 106

Climate, 42, 43, 50, 54–55, 59, 60, 61, 70, 91, 92
and development of color, 42–43, 54–55, 91, 92
and development of darker skins, 50, 59–61
and development of lighter skins, 61, 70
Colonialism and color, 88, 89, 99, 102, 103, 107, 117
See also: Imperialism
Color,
of eye, 12, 13, 14, 15, 16–17, 20–21, 60, 61
and vision, 15–17, 60, 61
and white of, 14, 15
in iris, 14–18, 61
in pupil, 14–17
in retina, 12, 17
of hair, 17–20
changes of, 18–21, 19
pigment of, 18–21
structure and, 18, 19
of skin,
and evolution, 36, 37, 42, 43, 51, 54, 55, 59, 60–61, 67, 70, 71, 72, 80, 81, 86, 87, 91
and heredity, 26, 28, 29, 31, 34, 36, 50–55
and vitamin D, 67, 70
and function, 14, 20, 21, 67, 70, 71
effect of thickness on, 8, 10, 12, 15
pigments of, 8, 9, 10, 12
variations of, 10, 12, 13, 21, 42, 75, 91
See also: Carotene, Chromosomes, Climate, Discrimination, Genes, Heredity, Man, Melanin, Migration, Mutations, Prejudice, Social selection, Sunlight, Tanning
Color discrimination. See Discrimination
Color line, 117, 119, 120
See also: Discrimination, Prejudice
Color prejudice. See Prejudice
Color and crime, 113, 114
Color and health, 110–114
Color and intelligence, 108–110, 114
Colour Act of 1926 (Apartheid), 99, 120, 122
Columbus, 86, 87–90
Communist Revolution, 91
Constitution of United States and color, 119

Costa Rica, 40–41
Cotton gin, 103

Da Gama, Vasco, 88
Declaration of Independence, 119
Discrimination, 93, 97, 98, 99, 106–108, 110–114, 118–121, 123
as law, 99, 107, 108, 118, 119, 122
See also: Negroes, Prejudice

Earth, curvature of, 43
East Indies, 89, 91
England, 39, 47, 86, 89–90, 93
Equality. See Man, equality of
Equator, 43, 61, 70, 86
Ergosterol, 70
Eskimos, 19, 86
Europe, 20, 27, 33, 37, 39, 43, 47, 55, 76–77, 79, 80, 81, 84, 86, 88–93, 98, 102, 106, 108, 118
Eye. See Color

Fiji Islands, 91
France, 79, 81, 84, 89, 90, 93
Freckles, 8, 11
See also: Melanin
French Revolution, 90

Genes, 34, 36, 37, 51, 61, 64, 97
for color, 28, 29, 31, 34, 50–55, 60, 67, 71, 86
functions of, 26, 28, 29
number of, 28, 29
See also: Chromosomes, Heredity, Mutations
Geneticists, 61
Genius and color, 110
Germany 86, 90, 91
Greece, 96
ancient, 92

Hair. See Color
Hausa, 56–57, 62–63
Hawaii, 91
Heredity, 25–34, 50–55, 60, 61, 97
See also: Chromosomes, Genes, Mutations
Holland, 76–77, 89, 90

Immigration and color. See Migration and color
Imperialism, 117
See also: Colonialism
Inca Indians, 89
Industrial Revolution. See Machine Age
Infrared radiation. See Sunlight
India, 42, 43, 87, 88, 89, 91

Indians, American, 13, *23*, 86, 87, 89, *88–89*
Intelligence tests, 108–110, 114
Iris. See Color
Israel, *45*, 80–81
Italy, 87, 89, 90

Japan, *6*, *66*, *74*, *82*, 91

Ku Klux Klan, 107

Latin America, 20, *38*, 40–41, 44, *71*, *78*, 86–89, 91, 92, 98, 107, 120
Lincoln, Abraham, 106

Machine Age, 37, 90, 106
Man,
    early, 39, 42, 50–55, 59–61, 70, 71, 72, 75, 86
        color of, 50, 59
        in New World, 86–90
        society of, 50–55, 61–64, 75
    equality of, 103, 107, 108–114, 117–123
    intermarriage of, 91–93
    mixing of color of, 29, 31, 88–93, 97, 98, 114, 117–120, 122, 123
    social classes of, 99, 102, 103
Malaysia, 91
Melanin (color pigment), 8, *9*, 10, *12*, 12–14, 15, 18, 19, 31, 36, 71, 111
    function of, 14, 15, 16, 17, 18, 21, 61, 70
Mexico, *78*, 91
Migration and color, 50–55, 67, 75, 86, 87
    and trade, 75, 80, 81, 86, 87, 88
    in modern times, 90, 91, 107, 108
    in New World, 86–90
Mongols, 80
Mulattoes, 120
Mutations, 31, 34, 39, 50–55, 60, 61
    See also: Chromosomes, Genes, Heredity, Migration

Natural selection, theory of, 50–55, 59, 60–64, 67, 70, 71, 97
    See also: Heredity, Social selection
Nazis, 108
Negroes, 91, 107, 108, *109*, 110–114, 117–121
    after Civil War, 107, 108, 110
    and slavery, 90, 102, 103, 106
    See also: Discrimination, Poverty and color, Prejudice
New York, New York, 93, *94–95*, *100*, 109, 112–113
Nigeria, *41*, *56–57*, *62–63*, 100, 111
North America, 20, *20*, 30, *32*, 36, *48–49*, 83, 85, 86, 87, 87–93, *88–89*, 98, *121*

Ottoman Empire, 87

Persian Empire, 80
Peru, 91
Philippines, 89, 91
Polynesia, 20
Portugal, 87–90
Poverty and color, 98, 99, 106, 108–114
    See also: Color and crime, Color and health, Color and intelligence
Prejudice, 93, 97, 98, 99, 107, 108, 110, 114, 117–123
    justifications of, 98, 106–108, 110, 114, 118, 122
    solutions to, 120–123
Pupil of eye. See color

Racism,
    among dark-colored peoples, 118
    among light-colored peoples, 106–108, 117–122
    See also: Discrimination, Prejudice, White Supremacy
Retina of eye. See Color
Rickets, 70, 71
    and childbirth, 70, 71
Roman Empire, 80, 92
Russia. See U.S.S.R.

Scandinavia, 20, 67, *73*, 90
Scotland, 19, 89
Segregation, 119, 120
    See also: Apartheid, Discrimination
Sex cells, 25, 26, 34
    See also: Chromosomes, Genes, Heredity
Slavery, 29, 31, 108
    and indenture, 90, 99, 102
    economic reason for, 99, 102, 103, 106, 107
    history of, 88–90, 99, 102, 103, 106, 107, 117
Social selection, 61–64, 71, 72, 96, 98
    See also: Natural selection
South Africa, 91, 99, 119, 120
Spain, 87–89

DISCARD

Sunburn. See Tanning

Sunlight, 14, 15–21, 36, 43, 59, 60, 61, 86,
  infrared radiation of, 14, 42, 43
  strength of, and color, 42, 43, 67, 70, 71, 72, 81, 97
  ultraviolet rays of, 14, 42, 43
  visible light of, 14, 42, 43
  See also: Color, Freckles, Tanning

Tanning, 14, 15, 36, 37, 59, 60, 61, 70, 86
  See also: Sunlight

Twins,
  fraternal, 34
  identical, 34

Ultraviolet rays. See Sunlight
UNESCO, 120
United Nations, 120, 121

  See also: Universal Declaration of Human Rights
United States, 40, 46, 48–49, 83, 85, 87, 88–89, 91, 92, 92–93, 94–95, 98, 100, 102–103, 103, 104, 105, 106–108, 109, 110, 111, 112–113, 115, 118, 118, 119, 120–121
Universal Declaration of Human Rights, 119, 121, 122
U.S.S.R., 72–73, 91, 93

Vitamin D and color, 70, 97
  See also: Rickets

West Indies, 90
"White man's burden," 107
  See also: White Supremacy
White Supremacy, 93, 98, 106–108, 117–120, 122

Zulu, 31

AUTHOR NOTES

ROBERT COHEN received his Master's degree from UCLA. He then became a television director for the U.S. Army, and served at NATO headquarters in Paris. Later, while studying for his doctorate in social psychology at the Sorbonne, he made a highly praised documentary on Red China for NBC and subsequently became one of the first Americans to visit the four major Communist capitals: Moscow, Peking, Cuba and East Berlin. He has since produced a number of prize-winning documentaries and made an international name for himself as a foreign correspondent.

KEN HEYMAN is, in the words of Edward Steichen, "the most important photographer to emerge in the last ten years." And his accomplishments have borne out the claim. In the past decade, his work has appeared in photographic annuals more often than that of any other photographer. His one-man shows have traveled throughout the world, and he has had important exhibits at the Smithsonian Museum and the Hallmark Gallery. He is best known, perhaps, for the picture book Family, *with a text by Dr. Margaret Mead, and* This America, *written by President Johnson.*

DR. JUAN COMAS is a noted anthropologist who has been involved in the fight against racial prejudice for many years. Born in Minorca, Spain, in 1900, he studied at the universities of Madrid and Geneva. Dr. Comas is a prolific writer in his field and his study of racial myths for UNESCO has been translated into fifteen languages. He was also an original member of the panel of experts who drew up the United Nations' Declaration of Human Rights. Dr. Comas is now head of the Section of Anthropology of the Institute of Historical Investigations of the National Autonomous University of Mexico.